The Highway Code for Marriage

Copyright © Michael and Hilary Perrott 2005

Published 2005 by CWR, Waverley Abbey House, Waverley
Lane, Farnham, Surrey GU9 8EP, England. Reprinted 2005, 2007
(twice), 2009.
Registered Charity No. 294387. Registered Limited Company No.
1990308.

The right of Michael and Hilary Perrott to be identified as the
authors of this work has been asserted by them in accordance
with the Copyright, Designs and Patents Act 1988.

All rights reserved. No part of this publication may be reproduced,
stored in a retrieval system, or transmitted, in any form or by
any means, electronic, mechanical, photocopying, recording or
otherwise, without the prior permission in writing of CWR.
See back of book for list of National Distributors.

Unless otherwise indicated, all Scripture references are from the
Holy Bible: New International Version (NIV), copyright © 1973,
1978, 1984 by the International Bible Society.

Concept development, editing, design and production by CWR.

Printed in Croatia by Zrinski

ISBN 978-1-85345-331-1

The Highway Code for Marriage

Michael & Hilary Perrott

CWR

Good marriages do not just happen.
   This is for you if you are thinking of:

O Getting married

O Giving up on your marriage

O Making your marriage even better

> **MYTH:**
> 'Love just happens; you can't help it'

In this handbook you will find:

O Marriage takes more than love (a lot more!)

O You get out of marriage what you put into it

O Prevention is better than cure

O The marriage that lasts for life

> **MYTH:**
> 'Problems mean you can't be right for
> each other'

Questions people ask:

O **'We're getting married. Can we be sure our
   love will last?'**

O 'We've almost given up. Is there any hope of saving our marriage?'

O 'We've got a good marriage but could it be even better?'

What follows has grown out of two people's search for each other. Their marriage began with misunderstanding and angry argument, until the very words 'I love you' became 'I hate you'. But they got one thing right – they never gave up, and they built a marriage better than their dreams.

They went on to spend thousands of hours counselling people from all walks of life, people who found that love is more than the 'wow' of romantic excitement or sexual attraction which can explode at first sight. That real love involves choices, self-sacrifice and determination. It is sensitive and unselfish. It can be injured – and revived.

In these pages they show that marriage is not just the sharing of four walls, a bank account and a bed. It can be the cold, dull, unstable relationship that the media so often describe, or a partnership like no other. Comrades in a battle, companions on a journey, best friends, mates to work with, lovers to enjoy.

Is this what you are looking for? You may want to read this handbook together, side by side, page by page, but some will find it easier to read separately, at their own speed, and then talk through the bits that apply to them. But read it all for it is on this sure foundation that marriage is built.

Read on and you will find good marriages do not just happen – they are made.

The seven secrets of a happy marriage are **Communication**, **Affection**, **Respect**, **Encouragement**, **Forgiveness**, **Unselfishness** and **Loyalty**. The first letters of the words spell **CAREFUL**, and the degree to which these are present in a marriage influences whether or not it thrives – or even survives. Although the authors of this handbook are committed Christians the principles outlined here can be followed by people of other faiths or none.

If you are not careful with your health you may fall sick and die. If you do not take care when driving or crossing the road you, or others, may be injured or killed. Without care the house becomes a ruin, the garden a wilderness, the farm unproductive and the business a failure. If you take care in every other department of life, then why not in marriage?

Read on – and enjoy your marriage.

CONTENTS

(9) **C**ommunication
brings light to your marriage
why some do not talk, tips for talking,
disagreeing but not disagreeable, learning to listen

(23) **A**ffection
brings warmth to your marriage
why some find it hard to show,
words and hugs, ten steps to good sex

(37) **R**espect
brings dignity to your marriage
deserve it, expect it and give it,
gender, personality and love languages

(53) **E**ncouragement
brings hope to your marriage
scrap the failure list, be generous with praise,
'I'm proud of you' works wonders

(63) **F**orgiveness
brings peace to your marriage
a choice not a feeling, not perfect yourself,
strength not a weakness, forgive or fester

(73) **U**nselfishness
brings joy to your marriage
money, time and habits, likes and dislikes,
roles and responsibilities, the chicken and the egg

(85) **L**oyalty
keeps love in your marriage
parents, children and friends, how affairs develop,
preventative measures, choosing to trust, to
stay or go

(101) Wrap up

(105) In the middle of a muddle

Communication
Affection
Respect

Encouragement

Forgiveness

Unselfishness

Loyalty

Communication

brings light to your marriage
why some do not talk, tips for talking,
disagreeing but not disagreeable, learning to listen

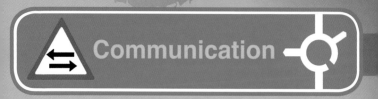

Communication

That means talking and listening to each other. Why? To understand and to be understood. In talking you bring your partner into your inner world, in listening you enter theirs. With talking and listening come understanding. What makes your husband tick. How your wife feels. The way you can meet each other's needs.

Any other reason? Yes, communication shows you care. You are interested in what she thinks. You care enough to ask … and care enough to listen. You listen to the hopes and the fears, you share sadness and joy. You make time for each other.

But …

He said, 'We don't argue, we just don't talk.'
She said, 'There's nothing to talk about!'
Why is that? Well, here are some …

Blocks to communication

O **Formative years.** How parents communicate with each other and their children can greatly influence their children's lives and marriages. But though the early years *explain* they do not *excuse*. You do not *have* to be silent like your father or shout like your mother. You have a choice.

O **Fear.** Are you afraid of appearing weak or stupid if you speak? You do not offer an opinion for you reckon it is better not to speak than be ridiculed or rejected. Or you avoid an angry outburst by not saying anything.

O **Peace at any price.** Anything to avoid conflict. Brush it under the mat. But 'Yes sir, no sir, anything you say, sir' creates a dictator and a doormat. There is peace of a kind but not respect for either doormat or dictator.

○ **Criticism**. Negative comments can leave you thinking, 'What's the use of talking? I'm always put down. Why bother?' Remarks like 'Talking to you is like talking to the wall', 'What a stupid idea', 'Rubbish' and 'Grow up, can't you?' may please the speaker but devastate the listener.

○ **Television**. Watching a programme together can be a time of sharing and gives stuff for communication, but when one person spends long hours in front of the box or computer, the other may feel 'he prefers it to me'. Then hurt becomes anger, anger withdrawal, and withdrawal silence.

○ **Bedtimes**. Go to bed at different times and you will probably get up at different times, so there is less communication at both ends of the day.

○ **Busyness.** If you are too busy to talk to each other or too busy to listen, you are too busy! If you are over-busy you will be overtired, and if you are overtired anger is more likely to be stirred up and conversation to dry up.

○ **Talkativeness**. If one person hogs the airtime the other will give up talking and, in the end, listening.

○ **Resentment**. Past hurts (distant or recent) are drawn into the present. As you remember you relive the pain. It is as if it is happening now. And then you let fly with bitter words or hold it in bitter silence. One couple had what they called 'ordinary huffs' which could last for hours, 'mega huffs' which could last for days, and sometimes 'super mega huffs' which could drag into weeks. Huffing and puffing are the opposite of talking and listening.

> ## MEMO
> **If you are too busy to talk to each other, you are too busy!**

TIPS FOR TALKING

This is what one husband says: 'We were so busy with the children, house and work, we weren't really talking except about the practicalities of living. So one day I got a bolt and put it on the inside of the kitchen door. After our evening meal I put the children in the next room and locked the door behind them. I went back to the table and had a second cup of tea with my wife. On the other side of the door civil war broke out, rapidly becoming less and less civil! But we pretended not to notice.

'After a while the kids got the hang of it and they gave us the space we needed so badly. We would have a second cup of tea and maybe a third. Perhaps 20 minutes. We talked about trivial things, what happened that day, who said what. But also we shared deep things, hurts and hopes, joys and fears. We laughed together. And the practice we started that day at the kitchen table became the habit of years, and was the basis of a marriage better than anything we ever dreamed of.'

○ **Make it a priority**. If you do not talk and listen to each other regularly you will never be really close, and without realising it you will grow further and further apart. Nothing is more important than communication for, as one wife put it, 'When my husband talks to me I feel more like a person.' Carve time out of your day. After your evening meal? When the children are in bed? With shift work it may have to vary. You will not *find* time, you have to *make* it, for there are always so many things which distract or disrupt.

Plan the time, then protect it. Turn off the phone. Occupy the kids.

You will not find time, you have to make it

MEMO

O **Make the effort**. It is not easy when you are tired, stressed or preoccupied, and when you just want to stop thinking. One determined husband said, 'I *want* to watch television, but I *will* talk with my wife.'

O **Ask questions**. 'What happened today? Funny things … hard things?' 'How do you think I should deal with this?' 'How are you feeling?' 'What would you like to do?' 'Any ideas?' Some people offer information readily, others need it drawn from them.

O **Share meals**. The word 'companionship' comes from the Latin, 'one who eats bread with another'. All over the world families talk and relax over their meals. Do not miss out on it. You can chew things over in more ways than one!

O **Share interests**. Be interested in each other's interests. If a hobby or a sport is important to him, make sure you know something about it. Try to understand his excitement. How can he talk to you about it if you do not have a clue? You may not be involved in an interest of hers, but ask questions until you have some notion of what it is about. The more interests you have in common the more communication there will be. How about a new activity you can enjoy together?

O **Share feelings**. Men talk easily in the realm of facts – margins of victory by the team, the cost of fuel – and that is part of communication. But to feel close a woman needs to be able to share feelings, hers and her husband's. Men in particular have to work hard to talk at this level. To express their hurts or hopes makes them vulnerable, but the sharing of feelings leads to trust and love.

O **Go to church together**. It has been wisely said, 'If you ever find a perfect church, don't join it, for as soon as you join it, it will cease to be perfect!' But it is undoubtedly true that a couple who worship together regularly, who aim to build their lives on the teachings of Christ, and enjoy the fellowship of like-minded people, will have a lot in common.

O **Go out together**. You spent time and money on your house or flat. You love it? But you need to get out of it – together. If day after day and month after month you never go out, the four walls that were such an achievement to get can seem more like a prison than a home. Go places, do things, with others, on your own. Get a baby-sitter. Going out widens your horizon and gives 'talk-about stuff'.

O **Go away together**. Holidays are a good investment in marriage and family life with the opportunity to relax away from home, though with children holidays may not be exactly islands of rest. But if a couple can manage to have a 'mini-moon' of 24 or 48 hours on their own, that can be fun to plan, fun to have and fun to look back on.

How about disagreements?

Must you win every argument? Then your victories are defeats! Defeat for *you*, for you lose your partner's respect, and if you continue to insist that you are right, you may lose their love. It is not disagreements that matter, it is how you handle them. How about this?

O **Openly**. Choose to share openly what you think and how you feel. Do not say to yourself, 'If he really loved me he would know what I want', for neither of you is a mind-reader. You need to say it like it is, and do not exaggerate. 'Never' and 'always' are seldom true. When listening, do not interrupt. Openness is easier when there is courtesy.

> **MYTH:**
> If he really loved me he would know what I want

O **Privately**. Choose the place. If criticism is needed, do it when no one else is present. Criticise in public and you will have an angry partner in private, who will not listen to what you are saying and, if change is needed, is less likely to change.

O **Gently**. Choose the words. 'I felt hurt …' is better than 'You hurt me …' for the first acknowledges pain but the second passes judgment. Use hard words and you make the task harder. 'Calling a spade a spade' can be a lame excuse for a crude attack. Opt for the gentler words; you are more likely to be heard. Instead of 'I totally disagree', how about 'I look at it this way'? You can disagree without being disagreeable. Words wound … or heal.

O **Quietly**. Choose the tone. People react so quickly and lose their temper so easily they feel they cannot help it. But it is not so. Anger rises with voice level and can be controlled by speaking quietly and calmly. Gentle words and tone are more likely to get gentle answers. Remember the saying, 'The more you shout the less I hear.'

○ **Honestly**. Choose the manner. There are two traps. The first is blame ('*You* make me mad') and the second is defensiveness ('*I* can't help it'). He sees himself as a victim and his wife as totally unreasonable. But she feels equally innocent. The truth may lie between the two. 'I honestly feel you were wrong, but I can see how I contributed to it. I'm sorry.'

○ **Lovingly**. Choose the position. It does not have to be a battle of wills. If there is something tricky to deal with, sit down together. Opposite sides of the table and there is a barrier, opposite ends of the room and there is distance. But beside each other, even though your lips may be saying something which is hard to accept, your arms are saying, 'I love you.'

○ **Practically**. Choose the time. Right now when *you* want to talk she may be too tired, or he too preoccupied, to really take it in. Or you might agree that if either of you feels that things are beginning to get out of hand, you can say, 'Let's leave it for the moment.' This is not an excuse for evading important issues, but at *this* moment if you continue there will be more hurt than progress. If necessary simply agree to disagree for it is far more important to be happy than to be right.

○ **Sensibly**. Choose the outcome. Ask 'Is it really worth arguing about this?' A year from now, a week from now, will it matter? The marriage matters more than the issue. Do not let disagreement divide or distance you. Determine to strengthen your relationship.

> ## It is not disagreements that matter, it is how you handle them

MEMO

Are you a good listener?

O Where do you look? One husband thought he was saving time because he read the newspaper, watched television and talked to his wife all at the same time. What she thought about that saving of time is not recorded. Where do you look? At her or past her? Give her your undivided attention. Look at her – except when you are driving! You listen with your eyes as well as your ears.

O What are you thinking? What you are going to say when he is finished? Then maybe you are not really listening.

O What are the feelings behind the words? Behind words there can be pain, pleasure or perplexity. What emotions can you hear behind these words?

- 'You spoke so sharply to me in front of our friends.'
- 'You've made so many promises.'
- 'I've just learned there are going to be redundancies.'
- 'I think I'm pregnant.'
- 'The children have been dreadful today.'
- 'I got the job.'

O When you do not understand. Ask 'Do you mean …?' or 'Are you saying …?' or 'Could you explain that again?' Do it at the time or, if that is not wise, do it later. It is important not only that you understand but also that your partner knows that you *want* to understand.

The three 'don'ts' of listening

O **Don't interrupt.** Interruption leads to raised voices (one voice trying to get on top of the other), frustration (at a broken train of thought) and anger (at selfish intrusion).

O **Don't dismiss**. Husband, if your wife is hurting it does not help to say, 'You shouldn't feel like that', or 'You'll be better tomorrow', or 'It doesn't matter'. Never make light of her feelings. Wife, if you say to him, 'You never listen', he will listen less for he knows it is not true. He does – sometimes! But when he does listen and you say, 'Thank you for listening to me', he is likely to listen more.

O **Don't advise**. Unless asked. Words like, 'This is what you should do' may not be what she needs. She may only want to be listened to. She may not actually (nine husbands out of ten do not understand this) want a solution! She just wants you to understand how she feels.

Odds and ends

O **Sex**. The verbal and sexual go together. A silent husband will eventually have an emotionally unresponsive wife. Then, of course, little sex can lead to even less talk. But the reverse is also true. Good sex warms the whole relationship, and the more sexual a wife becomes the more verbal a husband is likely to be.

O **Understanding**. You will open up more readily to each other if you feel understood. Study your mate. Her point of view. His strengths and weaknesses. Her likes and dislikes. How he deals with pressure. Her monthly cycle. What she wants most from him. What makes her feel special. Let your first aim be to understand each other and your second to be understood. Understanding opens the door to communication and communication the door to love.

Understand your roots. A husband was in the bathroom when he heard his wife calling, 'OK, Joe?' He bristled, 'Get off my back, woman.' Then he thought, 'Why did I react like that? She only asked if I were ready.' Suddenly he realised that when he was a boy his mother was never off his back – nag, nag, nag all day long. When he heard his wife's voice, in the depths of his being he had heard his mother's. Past pain affected present communication.

○ **Values**. If one person is passionate about truth and the other is comfortable with lies, then there will be major problems and ongoing conflict. *Interests* may vary in a marriage but *values*, particularly honesty and faithfulness, need to be the same. Work towards shared values – good ones.

○ **Being positive**. Negative attitudes and words close ears, hearts and lips, but compliments open them. Constructive criticism is more likely to be effective if you are generous with praise. 'Well done', 'That was a great help', 'You look lovely', 'Good decision!' It is easier to live with compliments than complaints.

There are psychologists who say that people need four positive comments for each negative one they receive. Some need ten! To those who have lived with negative influences, particularly in early life, being positive may not come naturally. But it is a choice and can become a very good habit.

O **Prayer**. By and large the old proverb is true: those who pray together stay together. No wonder, for if you can talk to the Lord together it helps you talk to each other. Experienced counsellors note that they rarely meet couples with serious marriage problems who regularly pray together.

O **Relaxation**. If you work too hard for too long both health and love can suffer. Workaholics cannot give their best to their partners. If the mind is tight words are more likely to wound than woo. Make space for non-work. Unwind the mind with a hobby. Choose to relax.

MEMO

Do not spoil an apology with an excuse

O **Apology**. Do not spoil an apology with an excuse. When there have been hard words or a strained silence it may be that a simple and sincere 'I'm sorry' will open the door to communication again.

Communication brings light to your marriage. Affection brings warmth …

Communication

Affection

Respect

Encouragement

Forgiveness

Unselfishness

Loyalty

Affection

brings warmth to your marriage
why some find it hard to show,
words and hugs, ten steps to good sex

Behind the many arguments one couple had were the very different experiences of early years. His parents parted when he was ten, and he grew up longing for the affection that he had known and then missed as a child. His wife had come from a home where she had been sexually abused. For her, affection was associated with shame and pain. So beneath the superficial arguments was this underlying tension, a young man longing for affection, and a young woman finding it difficult to give or receive.

Why some find it difficult to show affection

O **No model**. He never saw his father's arm around his mother. She never remembered her mother greeting her dad with a kiss. Or maybe the child grew up in a one-parent family and the father was either remote or absent.

O **No experience**. There was no memory of being held or hugged. For one woman who said, 'I can never remember being kissed or cuddled or even touched by my mother', touch felt strange.

O **Sexual abuse**. There was touch, but of the wrong kind. So to touch may be difficult or to be touched may seem dirty.

O **Hidden pain**. She felt rejected as a child and promised herself that no one would ever hurt her like that again. She built such a wall around

herself that nobody could get close. But then she was trapped behind her own wall and it was hard to break out.

O **Fear of being misunderstood.** A wife is reluctant to show affection to her husband because she thinks he will interpret it as a come-on for sex.

Affection can be shown in many ways.

Verbally

It is not just the words, it is the tone of voice, that make 'I love you' special. Saying it and hearing it helps keep love alive. A woman especially is a 'hearing' person and needs the reassurance it brings. Her husband needs to do better than one unromantic man who, when his wife told him she loved him, replied, 'And vice versa!' However, it is not always one-sided. A husband married for 20 years said, 'My wife's brilliant in every way and I know she loves me, but …' and he added wistfully, 'she's never once told me.'

For some couples it comes:

O **Readily**. They use words and ways of saying them they are familiar with. They don't have to think about it.

O **Gradually**. They create their own vocabulary of endearments or pet names. Some, like Winston Churchill, are unusual. He affectionately called his wife, 'Dear Cat', and she, equally affectionately, responded with 'Dear Pig'! The main thing is that the words used are heard with pleasure.

Physically

Everyone has the capacity to give and receive love even if for some it is buried very deep. One husband who struggled with showing his feelings described his wife as his 'kissing coach'. In the end he became as physically affectionate as she was. Aim at getting the balance right, neither starved of affection nor smothered by it.

A wife put it quaintly with,

There is an inside 'me' and an outside 'me'. If my husband were to withdraw physically from the outside 'me' then the inside 'me' would be devastated. But when he touches or holds the outside 'me' he touches the very core of my being. I can't describe how much physical affection means to the 'me' inside.

O **In private**. Holding hands, arm around the waist, a kiss, hug or cuddle, back scratched, hair ruffled, foot rubbed; what is specially enjoyable to one person may not be to the other. For one being stroked gives pleasure, while another finds it intensely irritating. You have to ask and tell. If a wife likes sitting close to her husband and with his background of wanting space he is uncomfortable, both are going to need sensitivity. Insist, and he feels invaded; push her away, and she feels rejected. He has to meet her need of closeness and she respect his need for space. But if you are determined to find a way, you will find it.

You decide *how* you show affection to each other and *when*. What do you do if your wife or husband comes to you for a hug and you do not feel like it? Well, if at that moment he needs it, give it. Not with a yawn, but with warmth. To do something you do not feel like doing is not hypocrisy but the generosity of love.

This bit is for husbands particularly. If the only time you show affection to your wife is as a prelude to sex, in the end she will feel, 'He wants it' rather than, 'He loves me'. The more non-sexual affection she enjoys with you – a hug for

a hug's sake with nothing else in view – the more she is likely to be responsive sexually. When she feels loved she feels more like loving.

○ **In public**. What is OK in private may not be in public. You do not want to embarrass each other or other people. Agree what words and touch you are both comfortable with when others are present. If a couple have children it is good that those children see their parents being (non-sexually) affectionate to each other.

Sexually

More space is given to the showing of affection sexually than the showing of it verbally or physically, not because these are not important but because the sexual is more complex.

Sex is not the creation of porn magazines but of God. Of human sexuality the Bible says, 'Male and female he created them', and then adds, 'God saw all that he had made, and it was very good' (Gen. 1:27,31). The intimacy it brings is such that Jesus said, 'The two will become one flesh,' and 'They are no longer two, but one' (Matt. 19:5,6).

TEN STEPS TO GOOD SEX

1. **Affection**. If you live in an *environment* of affection then the *events* of sex are far more fulfilling. Loving words and touch day by day help a wife feel loved. Husband, the more your wife feels loved by you the more she will enjoy sex, and the more she enjoys sex with you the more you will enjoy it! One husband said, 'The best thing for me in sex is my wife's obvious pleasure in it.' His wife explained, 'If you live in an *atmosphere* of affection as I do, *arousal*'s not difficult.'

2. **Understanding**. If you are a good cook or a computer operator you may have learned from

a cookbook or manual as well as by experience. Why should sex be different? A *full* understanding of sex does not normally come naturally. One couple testified, on reading a book years after they were married, 'It transformed sex for us in one week.'

Men and women are different sexually. It has been said (there are exceptions to this) that a man is like a light bulb: flip the switch and he is immediately turned on. A woman is more like an iron: flip the switch and she takes time to warm up. One frustrated husband grunted, 'In our house the iron's fused!'

MEMO

The most important sexual organ is the mind

A man is affected by what he *sees* and a woman more by what she *hears* and *feels*. So after a heated argument when peace finally reigns, a husband may want to make love to his wife. She thinks, 'The man's mad.' She cannot understand it. But it is easy. She is just as attractive as she was before the argument. She has not changed shape, and he is attracted by what he *sees*. But for the last hour she has *heard*, 'You're stupid, you're useless and it's all your fault', and she *feels* 'He can't love me.' So sex is the last thing she wants. Remember the most important sexual organ is the mind.

What about orgasm? For the great majority of men it comes easily and if there is a problem at all it tends to be that it comes too quickly. They need to learn control. There are women for whom the climax comes readily, but for others it is an art they learn. Whichever the case most women do not come to a climax through intercourse alone but need the stimulation of the clitoris. Some are never orgasmic yet thoroughly enjoy the intimacy of sex.

If a couple find it difficult to have intercourse, or in having it find it consistently painful, then they should seek professional help.

3. **Unselfishness**. What happens in bed is influenced by what happens out of bed. A husband who does not help in the house or with the children, or is glued to the TV or computer while his wife does all the chores, is guaranteed a sexually unresponsive wife. A wife who always has the last word and always wants her own way, in the long run will not have a loving husband. Selfishness ruins sex. If one is a giver and the other a taker, there will be conflict. If both are takers, there will be disaster. But with two good givers there is likely to be good sex.

Selfishness ruins sex

MEMO

The frequency of sex? There is no norm. It varies from couple to couple. It's affected by the monthly cycle, by pregnancy, sickness, anxiety, preoccupation, tiredness, age – and hormones. The rule for both husband and wife is: it should not happen *always when* you want it, nor should it happen *only if* you want it. The one can choose to control the urge, the other can choose to respond even when initially not in the mood. Unselfishness works wonders and moods can change. There has to be a meeting of minds as well as bodies. Between two unselfish people it is not difficult.

4. **Energy**. Tired minds and tired bodies do not make for good sex. Sex is important in marriage

and should not be left to the fag ends of time and energy. Spontaneity in sex is great, but in busy lives it is all too easy for it not to happen. Sex is much more likely to take place within the framework of protected time and energy. The secret in saying 'yes' to each other is saying 'no' to other things which crowd the time and drain the energy. Prioritise.

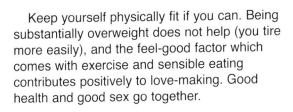

MEMO

The secret in saying 'yes' to each other is saying 'no' to other things

Keep yourself physically fit if you can. Being substantially overweight does not help (you tire more easily), and the feel-good factor which comes with exercise and sensible eating contributes positively to love-making. Good health and good sex go together.

5. **Openness**. If you are thinking of getting married, be open about the past. The facts, perhaps not too many details if painful to speak of or painful to hear. If you were abused when you were young it is best to share it with your husband or wife (or husband- or wife-to-be). They will not reject you and will have much greater understanding if you have difficulties arising from the past.

Be open about your love-making. What helps or hinders. What touch where. When something is all right and when it is not. Sex is not always fabulous, sometimes it is quite ordinary and sometimes it does not seem to work at all. Wife, if you pretend, then he will never know what is best for you, and you will build up resentment inside yourself when he keeps getting it wrong.

Husband, be warned that what turns her on one day may turn her off the next. One very sexually contented wife laughed, 'I'm not being awkward, I'm just being a woman! I don't blame my husband for not understanding me, I don't always understand myself!'

6. **Time**. When it comes to sex the difference between men and women has been likened to the difference between football and a concert. The husband's natural instinct is to score a goal as quickly as possible, but his wife's enjoyment is found in the whole concert. Foreplay is not just 'the warm-up before the game' but an integral part of the sexual experience.

One couple's relationship left the wife disappointed and frustrated. She never came anywhere near being fulfilled. When asked by a counsellor how long the love-making took, the husband answered, 'About five minutes'. He had not realised that his wife needed, both physically and emotionally, more than that. There followed a significant improvement in sex for them which he explained with (tongue in cheek), 'I bought a clock and put it on the bedroom wall. I keep one eye on the clock!'

Just as a wife, like the iron, normally takes time to warm up, so she takes time to cool down, or come down from her peak of excitement. For her the afterglow is an important part of the love-making. If her husband immediately turns over and goes to sleep, she can feel used or rejected. He needs to hold her while her afterglow quietly subsides.

7. **Gentleness**. Be gentle with each other's bodies. Strong hands are OK, rough hands (with some work it is hard to avoid) maybe not be so OK. Calluses and caressing may not go well together. As a husband do not be rough with your wife; you can be passionate without inflicting pain.

One wife described her loving husband as 'tough and tender'.

Be gentle with each other's feelings. If there is some kind of love-making that your wife has difficulty with, respect her feelings about it. Do not insist and perhaps she may change later. If one day things have not gone well sexually, do not hold a post mortem on the spot. It is not a time for criticism but for support and encouragement. Talk about it later and let there never be ridicule.

Be gentle about pregnancy. If a woman is afraid of becoming pregnant she may be turned off sex. Agree about what contraception is best for you both. If you are not sure about which method, get professional advice.

Be gentle with each other if no children come. About one couple in ten do not have children, usually because of some medical condition. The yearning to be a mother or father can be intense and blame does not help when there is pain.

8. **Variety**. Variety is the spice of life – and to some degree of sex also. Some 'sexperts' say there are 95 possible sexual positions, but for many of these you would have to be an Olympic gymnast! Most couples use a number of methods which experience shows work for them but, whatever you do, do not settle for boredom. In bed, out of bed. Light, half-light or darkness. Naked or clothed. Morning, daytime or night. Perfume or music. A few minutes or a couple of hours. Men tend to look for variety more than women and women more for atmosphere than men.

Avoid pornography. It seldom does much for a woman. It may excite a man – initially, but it becomes addictive so he wants more and more explicit material to provide the same arousal. In the end it destroys the very desire it was supposed to waken. It is unrealistic nonsense and the ruin of relationship. If you want love, do not buy into porn. If you use the Internet, consider paying a small fee to one of the organisations which block millions of pornographic sites. Have a clean screen.

Many a husband feels undesired and even unloved because his wife seldom or never initiates love-making. There can hardly be a husband in the world who does not feel more of a man when his wife unashamedly shows that she wants him. Do it – at least sometimes. And do not be too subtle about it. Cooking his favourite meal is not likely to be a sexual come-on for him. He has eyes – make sure he uses them.

9. **Cleanliness**. The rhinoceros has been hunted because it is believed that a powder made from its horn is a powerful aphrodisiac. Far better than rhino horn is soap and water. Bad smells do not make for good sex. One couple struggled sexually because the husband never (actually never) washed his feet. When he took off his shoes and socks at bedtime, passion went out of the window.

Is there bad breath? Go to the dentist or doctor. Is there smoky breath? Give it up (unless you both smoke and one smell cancels out the other). Are there dirty hands and nails? Wash them. Is there BO? Have a bath or shower. Good hygiene is not only healthy but is a positive help in love-making.

10. **Privacy**. A lock on the bedroom door is one of the best aids to love-making. A small voice beside the bed, 'Daddy, what are you and Mummy doing?' does not help concentration. There is clear evidence that children are harmed by seeing their parents engaged in sex, and they can be disturbed by sound as well as sight. Couples with families need time and place so that they can be uninhibited in sharing their sexual love. Sometimes it might be while

the children are out. Lock the door, close the curtains, turn off the phone, turn up the music, do whatever is necessary to have privacy. Sometimes a couple are more conscious of the verbal than the physical, or the physical than the sexual, but all three combine to bring about the closeness which is at the very heart of a good relationship.

Affection brings warmth to your marriage. Respect brings dignity ...

Communication
Affection
Respect
Encouragement
Forgiveness

Unselfishness

Loyalty

Respect

brings dignity to your marriage
deserve it, expect it and give it,
gender, personality and love languages

Respect

In the New Testament the one thing that both wives and husbands are called upon to show to each other is respect. In Ephesians 5:33 it says, 'The wife must respect her husband,' and in 1 Peter 3:7 'Husbands … be considerate as you live with your wives, and treat them with respect.' How do you go about it?

O **Work on self-respect**. At the root of how you relate to others is how you see yourself. One wife had been very critical of her husband. Through counselling she came to see that she had 'let herself go' physically and was taking out on him her frustrations with herself. As she changed her habits of eating and exercise her new good self-image transformed her attitude towards him.

O **Deserve respect**. If you are 'a street angel and house devil' you will not deserve respect. What you are as a person greatly influences the attitude of your partner towards you. Kindness, honesty, fairness, unselfishness, self-control, warmth: if these things show in your life then you will probably have the respect you long for.

O **Expect respect**. Do not be a doormat. The doormat does not respect himself and in the end resents the dictator. Anyway no one in his right mind really wants a partner who is always compliant. If you feel your partner is not showing you respect, you should say so. You do not have to be aggressive to be assertive. Both of you should remember that if you have children, then the way in which you show respect to each other will be a model for them.

O **Give respect**. A wife came to recognise the effect her nagging had had on both her and her husband. He was no better and she was more bitter. Then she began to look for the good things in him and found more than she expected. In every way she let her growing respect be known, heard and felt by him. Instead of complaints there were compliments. There was dignity instead of dismissiveness. It took him a while to adjust to the new atmosphere in their home, but then his attitudes to her changed dramatically as he began to feel his wife's respect. He explained that he wanted to be the man 'she saw me to be'.

You show respect by what you say

O **Avoid jokes with a jag**. You may think it fun to have a dig at him, but if it hurts him is that really funny? Sarcasm says more about the speaker than the one at whom it is aimed.

O **Avoid language that offends**. If there are words which upset her, why use them? Dropping a couple from your vocabulary is not a sign of weakness but of strength.

O **Be positive about his interests even if they are not yours**. Ask questions. Learn enough so that he likes talking to you about the things he enjoys.

O **Be tolerant of minor flaws or faults; you have a few of your own**. Correct her in a lot of small things and she is more likely to reject a challenge in more important issues.

O **Never compare your partner unfavourably with an ex-husband or wife or partner**.

O **Be polite**. Words like 'please' and 'thank you' are always welcome.

○ **Lay off your in-laws**. In having a go at her family she may feel you are having a go at her. Unless of course she shares your views!

You show respect by how you listen

○ **Give full attention when he is speaking to you**. He will be more encouraged by your face than your back. If he has your eyes he will be reasonably sure he has your ears.

○ **Accept her feelings whether you understand them or not**. Her feelings are just as real to her as yours are to you.

○ **Respect his opinions even if you do not share them**. Rubbish his opinions and he will feel you are rubbishing him. Do not assume that the way *you* see things is the only way.

○ **Accept that when she talks about problems you are listening to feelings and not (necessarily) to complaints**. A husband said, 'I used to feel overwhelmed, and was probably defensive, when my wife started talking about problems. Then I realised that she just wanted to share her feelings with me, and I felt that I was a lucky man – well, most of the time!'

You show respect by what you do

○ **Courtesy**. How this is shown varies from person to person but everyone wants it.

○ **Telephone if you are going to be late**. It saves burning dinners or climbing walls.

○ **Tidiness**. If you like making work by your untidiness, try tidying it yourself.

O **Gentleness**. Violence destroys respect more rapidly than anything else. A woman can live in a prison in her own home, sometimes for years. All too often she is so ashamed or frightened that she says nothing to anyone. But by doing nothing her husband is able to continue his violent behaviour. The law exists to protect her and she should not hesitate to use it.

If you as a husband find yourself losing control and becoming violent you had better stop *now*. If you cannot, then you should get professional help *now*. You have probably already lost your wife's respect, but if you go on you may lose her, your home and even possibly your liberty. (It can, of course, be a woman who is violent.)

You show respect by how you look

O **Appearance**. Do you take care of your appearance out of respect for your partner? Face, figure, hair, dress? Are you making the best of yourself for your partner? These things do matter in a marriage.

O **Cleanliness**. Kissing bad breath is tough going; so is hugging BO. Dried sweat is not the best aftershave.

Respect the gender differences

These differences are *not absolute* male/female characteristics but are sufficiently common that husbands and wives should know and respect them. Understanding yourself as well as your partner goes a long way to preventing problems.

MAN

 WOMAN

MAN	WOMAN
He needs to feel *significant*, that he is adequate and respected.	She needs to feel *secure*, that she is loved, understood and cared for.
When bothered, he tends to think *silently*.	When bothered, she tends to be *open* about what is bothering her.
He *stops* talking to work out what he really wants to say.	She *starts* talking to work out what she really wants to say.
His communication is often *direct*: what he says is what he means.	Her communication may be *indirect*: with a hidden or suggested meaning.

Because of gender differences you are bound to misunderstand each other – for the first 25 years! Here are a couple of examples:

 MAN

 WOMAN

MAN	WOMAN
She asks, 'How did it go?' He says, 'Fine.' He means, 'Thanks for asking. It all went well. I have no problems, but I'm tired. It's nice to be home.'	She feels shut out and thinks, 'He doesn't want to share with me. That shows he doesn't care for me and if he doesn't care for me, does he really love me?'

What he says is true; it was 'fine', but her question was an invitation to talk and he has not responded to that. He gave her a skeleton when she needed a body.

WOMAN	MAN
'We're *always* in a hurry.' She means, 'I feel terribly pressurised today for there's so much to do. I wish we had time just to be together. I'd like to go out with you. Right now I'm feeling miserable and I need a hug.'	He thinks, 'What she's really saying is that if I did more she wouldn't be so stressed. She doesn't seem to notice all I do for her. And it's simply not true, we're *not* always in a hurry.'

She did not really say what she meant, so he took her literally and misunderstood.

MALE MISTAKES

The worst mistakes a husband can make when he tries to help or comfort his wife are to:

O **Offer a solution** (unless asked). She wants above all else that her husband understands her feelings and she may need *sympathy* more than *solutions*.

O **Dismiss her feelings**. It does *not* make her feel better to be told, 'It's no big deal' or 'It's not worth talking about'. He may think she is overreacting, but his 'Why get upset over a thing like that?' can make her feel worse. What is important to her, whether you understand it or not, is important.

FEMALE FAULTS

The worst faults of a wife as she tries to help or support her husband are to:

O **Demand that he talk**. A concerned wife sat down in front of her husband and said, 'Now talk!' His mind slammed shut! Request OK, demand not OK.

O **Direct what he should do**. 'You ought to …' makes him feel like a small boy being instructed by his mother. 'Do you think that …?' is better than 'You ought …' Questions are better received than directions.

> **MEMO**
>
> **What is important to her (or him), whether you understand it or not, is important**

GENDER GENERALITIES

O **Faces and feelings**. As a woman listens her face may mirror the feelings of the other person: sadness, joy, fear, perplexity. Men's feelings are no less deep than women's but generally their faces do not reveal them as much. So a wife may wrongly interpret that an impassive face means an unfeeling heart.

O **Lips and thoughts**. For many a woman (not all) talking is often part of the thinking process. What comes from her lips is not necessarily a conclusion but an examination of possibilities.

She sorts as she talks. But many a man does his thinking before he speaks. There is self-talk inside his head which leads to conclusions before he opens his lips. In general terms it might be said that women think aloud and men talk silently!

Women think aloud, men talk silently!

MEMO

Respect the personality differences

O **Opposites attract**. You may have been drawn to each other by your differences. The strong, quiet man and the bubbly girl met each other's needs. But then you find that …

O **Opposites attack** and when you want quietness she is bubbling and cannot understand why you do not respond. Gradually you come to understand that when …

O **Opposites accept** the differences in each other, it is much more enjoyable than being married to a replica of yourself.

What follows is *not* a formal analysis of personality but *some* of the characteristics which you may share or in which you may differ. Each person has two hands but you tend to use one more than the other. Everyone is both objective and subjective but you tend to be more one than the other – maybe 90 per cent more! Here are some examples.

THINKING

STEP BY STEP	JUMP BY JUMP

One husband says, 'I think in straight lines, step by logical step, left right, left right, cause effect, cause effect, plod, plod. My wife doesn't (always) think in straight lines. We're talking together when suddenly she comes out with something which bears no relation to what she said two seconds ago. How she got there is beyond me. So I go plod, plod, plod till I catch up with her, only to discover she can't understand why *I* changed the subject! I'm a plodder, she's a jumper. My plodding and her jumping used to drive us both crazy, but now we fall over laughing when we realise what's happening. Our respect for each other means that our differences delight rather than divide.'

TALKING

THE WOOD	THE TREES
You paint a broad picture giving an overall impression of what happened and what you experienced.	You paint the twigs and leaves – details of who was there, what they said, how they were dressed, their hobbies, friends and ancestry.

RELATING

OUTGOING	RESERVED
You have no difficulty in getting to know people and initiate conversation readily with your 100 closest friends!	You are quiet, and respond to rather than initiate conversation. You do not reveal personal details easily.

RELAXING

UNWIND WITH PEOPLE	UNWIND AWAY FROM PEOPLE
A husband comments, 'When my wife is tired she likes to be with a bunch of people and she recharges her batteries that way. When I'm tired I like to go for a walk in the park with a bag over my head!'	

WORKING

PERFECTIONIST	NON-PERFECTIONIST
Motto: 'If something's worth doing, it's worth doing well.' Do not start unless you are sure it will be 100 per cent right.	Motto: 'Let's get going.' That means the easiest and fastest way possible.

A wife laughed (sort of), 'My husband is brilliant at DIY and I asked him to fix the cupboard. He did –

three years later. He was trying to work out all that time the best way of doing it. When he did it, it took him five minutes.'

PLANNING

IN ADVANCE	LAST MINUTE
Information gathered, instructions read, clothes listed, timetable studied. Make plans and stick to them.	Motto: 'It will all work out.' You fly by the seat of your pants or go with the flow.

ARGUING

GENERAL	SPECIFIC
Feelings are expressed and generalisations made. An emphasis on facts is seen as nitpicking.	Things are black and white, true or false. 'Stick to the facts' is the motto.

Learn to respect your differences; they are part of what brought you together. One wife said, 'The more I understand him the more I respect him, and the more I respect him the more I love him.'

Respect the 'language' differences

It has been pointed out by Gary Chapman in his book *The Five Love Languages* that people tend to express love in five different ways: time, touch, words, gifts and actions. If two people do not understand each other's 'love languages' they are going to have problems, so it is important that you are able to recognise yours and that you understand theirs.

○ **Language of time**. This means listening to each other, looking at each other and doing things together even if it means doing nothing. Whatever the activity may be it is giving undivided attention and enjoying each other's company. Motto: Time together.

○ **Language of touch**. For some people touch gives pleasure and security in a way that nothing else does. Touch – which includes the sexual, but is far more than that – leads to the very core of their being. Motto: Touch me touch my heart.

○ **Language of words.** You express to your wife or husband the things you like about them. *Their* affirmation of *you* warms your heart, and *their* confidence and self-esteem is built up by what *you* say to them. Motto: Words warm hearts.

○ **Language of gifts**. For some a gift is just a thing given perhaps out of custom or duty, while for others it is the giver's way of saying, 'You're special to me and I love you', and it is received like that. Motto: The giver is in the gift.

○ **Language of actions**. Cooking, washing, cleaning, mending, changing the baby, taking the kids to school – all of which require planning, time and energy – are deeds which for some speak louder than words and say emphatically, 'I love you.' So is holding down a job and converting long hours at work into provision for the family. Motto: Doing is loving.

Below is a table filled in by a couple who only had one 'language' in common, but in coming to understand the differences between them came to an even deeper respect and closeness.

WIFE	LANGUAGES OF LOVE	HUSBAND
1	Language of time	3
2	Language of touch	2
5	Language of words	1
4	Language of gifts	5
3	Language of actions	4

Suggestion: Take this table and starting with a 1 beside your main love language go down to your least important with 5. Do it on your own and then compare with your partner. It may help you more than you imagine to understand each other.

Respect brings dignity to your marriage. Encouragement brings hope …

Communication
Affection
Respect
Encouragement
Forgiveness

Unselfishness

Loyalty

Encouragement

brings hope to your marriage
scrap the failure list, be generous with praise,
'I'm proud of you' works wonders

What everyone likes to receive – and needs to give.

A very experienced counsellor reported that he had never known a marriage breakdown where husband and wife were determined encouragers of each other. Not only do such marriages survive, they thrive. This is how it works.

You encourage by what you say

What you think about you are more likely to talk about. Now the Bible says expressly, 'Whatever is true, whatever is noble, whatever is right, whatever is pure, whatever is lovely, whatever is admirable – if anything is excellent or praiseworthy – think about such things' (Phil. 4:8). If every wife and husband made this the pattern of their thinking then their speaking would be the same.

A valid criticism is more likely to be received if you are also generous with praise. It is not only much more effective than nagging in bringing about change, but is also the best way of helping to maintain that change as a habit. People who feel encouraged *want* to be better and feel they *can* be. So be positive to your wife, give your husband praise. Not flattery, not things that are not true, but focus on the good you see. Be specific if possible. 'I like that top …' 'That's a great idea …' 'You did that well.'

ABOUT HOW THEY LOOK

There is something in your partner's face or figure or hair or dress that you like? If you see it, say it. If you do not do so, somebody else may. So let the compliment come first from you. If weight is a problem for your wife be specially encouraging. 'You look like a stuffed turkey' is crude, cruel and leads to comfort-eating. But encouraging words about how she looks give motivation to tackle the problem.

ABOUT HOW THEY ARE

○ **As a partner**. A wife complained, 'He always has a long list of my failures'. If you have that kind of list, scrap it. Tell her the things you admire in her, the reasons why you are glad you married her. Tell him how much you enjoy living with him – and why. 'I'm proud of you' works wonders.

'I'm proud of you' works wonders

MEMO

○ **As a lover**. No area is more sensitive than the sexual. If a man feels he is a failure in bed, he feels a failure. No one gets it right all the time. Nothing is more wonderful for a man than his wife's enjoyment of his love-making. Let him know it. A woman whose husband thinks she is great in bed and says so, is more likely to *be* great in bed.

○ **As a parent**. 'That was a tough situation. You handled it really well.' 'Thanks for helping out with the children: I couldn't have done it on my own.' 'The kids are proud of you.' Most parents want the best for their children and yet are all too well aware of the mistakes they make. Encourage-ment helps them redouble their efforts.

○ **As a homemaker**. Compliment the cook when something tastes good and the cook will make more of the same – or better. If there are children, be realistic about the state of the house. Notice the house when it is sparkling, not when it is untidy, and it is more likely to go on sparkling.

O **As a provider**. There are jobs which are too demanding and jobs which are not demanding enough. There are those who like what they work at and those who do not. But whatever the case they are helping to provide for the home. Do not take it for granted.

O **As a person**. Integrity, dependability, generosity, unselfishness – if any of these qualities are true of your wife or husband make sure they know you see it. If there has been a particular generous or unselfish act, then say so. Compliments do not make character but they certainly help it grow.

O **Say it in writing**. You are not Shakespeare but you are you, and you know best what will encourage your partner. A husband away from home opened his case and found a cryptic note, 'Remember Friday night?' A wife opened the coffee jar and a found a tiny ball of paper which, when unrolled, declared, 'You're a star!' A note, a card or a letter can be treasured for years.

O **Say it about them when they are present**. A newly married husband and wife were asked by friends how things were going. The husband patted his stomach laughingly with, 'I only have one problem, she's far too good a cook.' She glowed with pleasure. A husband retrained himself after retirement by going to computer courses and sitting his first examinations in more than 45 years. He admitted his pride when his wife told friends, in his presence, of the distinctions he had gained.

O **Say it about them in their absence**. 'I was talking to your husband recently,' a friend told her, 'and he mentioned what a great job you had done.' She felt warm inside when she heard what her husband had been saying about her.

Question: Why is it that some people have difficulty in receiving praise?

Answer: It is usually either because they are not used to it or because they do not think they deserve it. These two can be linked. If in early years the influences were negative – 'You're no good …' 'Why do you never do anything right?' You're more trouble than you're worth' – the child (now adult) sees himself as bad or stupid, and feels instinctively that any praise is untrue and is possibly being used to manipulate.

You encourage by what you do

O **Helping**. In the whole history of criminology it has never been known for a wife to murder her husband while he was washing the dishes or tidying the house. When a husband shares the chores his wife feels he is saying, 'I like sharing our home with you.'

O **Supporting**. Many speak warmly of their 'better halves'. Focus on each other's strengths, give support in each other's weaknesses. Redundancy can be devastating and with unemployment can come the feeling, 'I'm not wanted' or 'I'm no good'. It is great to know that even if the whole world is against you, one person is for you. Out of encouragement flows courage.

O **Organising**. There are haphazard homes which are happy, but generally chaos and conflict are not far apart. Organisation makes for freedom.

The shopping is done, the car is serviced, the baby-sitting arranged, the holiday planned, the bills paid. More gets done in less time, so there is less pressure and more time for enjoyment.

MEMO

Out of encouragement flows courage

O **Giving**. For one person there is little significance in gifts. For another there is a great deal, whether it comes as a surprise or whether it is long planned and eagerly awaited. A husband, vaguely aware that flowers grew in the ground, uncharacteristically thought he would surprise his flower-conscious wife. She told how she came into the house one day to find on a table a small vase in which there was a solitary dandelion. Underneath a note read, 'Will this do for starters?' She was thrilled. When it comes to gifts thought matters more than size.

O **Sharing**. One couple rarely did anything together until they embarked on a joint project. 'The time we spent together, the tears and the laughs that we shared, the conversations, on occasion late into the night, transformed our lives. What we *did* together *brought* us together in a way we could not have imagined.'

O **Initiating**. 'For years,' she said, 'anything other than the routine or predictable was always initiated by me. There was no fun unless I made it, and because I had to make it, it was not that much fun. Whatever got into him I do not know, but now he takes the lead and there are all kinds of surprises. The biggest surprise is himself!'

○ **Remembering**. Birthdays, anniversaries and Valentine's Day carry varying degrees of meaning. A wife cried, 'There was no card, nothing, on our anniversary. It was like a slap in the face.' His explanation: 'I forgot.' Her interpretation: 'He doesn't love me.' To be remembered is to be encouraged.

> ## To be remembered is to be encouraged
>
> MEMO

You encourage by what you are

○ **Comforting**. Who has not known disappointment, loss, illness, failure, loneliness or pain and has not longed for a listening ear or a shoulder to cry on? What wife is not grateful for her husband 'being there' for her through premenstrual tension or the trying symptoms of menopause? When things are hard the best medicine may be a hug. To know that how you feel will never be trivialised or ridiculed is wonderfully reassuring. Everything falling to pieces around you but she (or is it he?) is by your side. Love like that is one of life's greatest strengths.

○ **Laughing**. If you do not take yourself too seriously and can laugh at yourself, that makes for a good relationship. If you laugh at your partner in a playful way (and only as long as they like it), that can be fun. But laughing together (at whatever) is one of the best ways of relaxing, and many couples find that tension is dissolved by laughter.

○ **Appreciating**. You may not be able to change the situation but you can change your attitude to it. The positive 'half full' is always better than the negative 'half empty.' To live with a complaining, fault-finding grumbler is, as one person put it, 'Like tearing the flesh off my bones'. It is easy to live in an atmosphere of appreciation so cultivate an attitude of gratitude.

○ **Confiding**. A person moving to a new locality was advised that there were two ways of advertising. The first was an ad in the paper, the second was to tell _____ in strictest confidence. The recommendation was, 'Go for the second. It takes a little longer for the news to get around, but it is just as effective and the service is totally free!' But in marriage a betrayal of confidence is no laughing matter. To be able to confide your secrets, your fears or failures, and know beyond a shadow of a doubt that what you have said is secure, encourages you to go on being open and transparent.

○ **Protecting**. The physical strength of her husband helps a woman feel safe, and sometimes that strength may actually have to be used. But a man, as well as a woman, needs to feel safe emotionally. To know, come what may, there is one person who will always stand up for you. Your reputation as well as your person is safe in their hands.

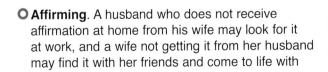

MEMO

Cultivate an attitude of gratitude

○ **Affirming**. A husband who does not receive affirmation at home from his wife may look for it at work, and a wife not getting it from her husband may find it with her friends and come to life with them. Nothing builds self-esteem as much as the generous and on-going affirmation of one's mate.

Encouragement brings hope to your marriage. Forgiveness brings peace ...

Communication

Affection

Respect

Encouragement

Forgiveness

Unselfishness

Loyalty

Forgiveness

brings peace to your marriage
a choice not a feeling, not perfect yourself,
strength not a weakness, forgive or fester

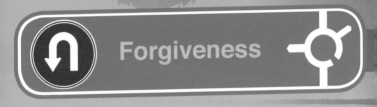

A man told his friend, 'Whenever my wife and I have an argument she becomes historical.'

'You mean hysterical,' the friend replied.

'No, I mean historical. She reminds me of everything I ever did!'

Hurts become deeper when memories become longer.

Little everyday injuries are so trivial we hardly notice that we forgive or are forgiven. He treads on her toe and says, 'Oh, sorry!' and she replies, 'That's all right.' It was not deliberate. It hurt for only a few seconds. It is never referred to again and they both forget about it. Unthinkingly she lets out a sharp word. He feels a momentary prick of pain, but he realises she is under pressure and makes no comment. He does not think about it and after a few days there is no hurt and soon no memory.

But what happens when there is a really big hurt? Every time you think about it you smoulder inside. It may have been a single act or the collective weight of a hundred small grievances. The anger does not go away. It grows into a long-term resentment that you have been treated this way. You feel you have been let down, embarrassed, deceived, betrayed. Your anger may be red-faced and loud-voiced or it may be as cold and hard as ice. There is a wall of bitterness between you. How can you forgive? Anyway, what is forgiveness?

What forgiveness is not

O **Condoning**. Forgiving him does not mean you approve of what he did.

○ **Forgetting**. Forgive and forget? If the offence is small, yes, you will probably forget all about it. But if it is big you may never forget even if you forgive.

○ **Denying**. For some the pain is too great to take on board and so they deny, not only to others but to themselves, that it happened at all.

○ **Pretending**. You will not admit to anyone that you are hurting and you claim everything is fine, but the fact that you are not shouting or screaming does not mean that you are not angry.

○ **Losing**. The person who forgives is not necessarily the loser. Forgiving may be winning.

What forgiveness is

○ **Choosing, not feeling**. If you have been badly hurt, forgiving may be the last thing you feel like doing. Fortunately forgiveness has very little to do with feelings and everything to do with choice. Just as you choose to talk when you would rather be silent, to be kind when to do so would be an effort, to be unselfish when the opposite is much more attractive, so forgiveness is more a choice than a feeling.

> ## Forgiveness is more a choice than a feeling
>
> MEMO

The Christian teaching is clear. Colossians 3:13 says, 'Forgive whatever grievances you may have against one another' and then goes on with the example of Jesus, 'Forgive as the Lord forgave you.' Forgiveness is a command, a standard and a choice.

○ **Choosing not to dwell on the hurt**. You cannot help the thought coming into your mind; bang, it is there, uninvited and unwelcome. But you are responsible for what you allow your mind to dwell on. The more you rehearse the hurtful words or deeds the more indelible they become in your mind.

○ **Choosing not to talk about it**. If you talk about it, you think about it. If you think about it, you feel it. If you feel it, it will hurt you. Each time you remind your wife how she hurt you, you hurt her – and yourself.

○ **Choosing not to retaliate**. Justice may say, 'An eye for an eye' – 'If you do that to me, I'll do it to you.' Forgiveness says, 'I could, but I won't.'

○ **Choosing to let it go**. Some people find it particularly hard to let go past hurt but in the end it is a choice. One wife wrote, 'I used to replay the video tapes of what he said and did, over and over in my mind. Then one day I let it all go and I was free.'

○ **Choosing to go on choosing**. One husband, when he forgave his wife for her unfaithfulness, said, 'I felt all the pain go away.' But later he began to replay the tapes in his mind and to cast it up to her, and all the pain came back again. He 'unforgave'. Forgiving is not only a one-off act but also an ongoing attitude.

Reasons for forgiveness

○ **You are not perfect yourself**. Take a look inside: an honest look. If others knew the whole truth about you, what would they think? She said, 'I was hurt by what he did but if I'm really honest I have to admit that I'm not much better, and in some ways maybe worse.'

Harmony. Gripes, grudges and grunts. 'You hurt me, I'll hurt you', by withdrawal, by silence, by whatever. Heated exchanges or cold coexistence. One couple admitted, 'Our silence was exhausting!' The 'get-even' policy locks you into the past. But who wants to go on living like that? Forgiveness creates the attitude necessary to making a new beginning. It allows a couple to move on together.

Peace of mind. What the mind looks for it usually finds. If it looks for hurt it will find hurt. Do you, as a husband, have a list of her failings and can recall the tiniest detail? Have you stuffed all her faults into a cupboard so that if the door were suddenly opened they would all spill out? One wife confessed, 'I have a drawer full of wriggling resentments.' You have a straight choice: pain or peace. Hold on to the hurt and it corrodes everything. Replay it in your mind, over and over, and the pain will grow and perhaps become hate. Let the hurt go, and though it may take time, the pain will go. It's forgive or fester. Forgiveness is for the forgiver as much as for the forgiven. Refusing to forgive is like shooting oneself in the foot.

Healthy mind and body. Inner stress may take its toll on the body. Keep your anger alive, refuel it by what you think and say, and you could end up with broken sleep, chest pains, ulcers, headaches, depression and maybe a breakdown. Every doctor knows patients whose conditions are made worse by gnawing resentment inside.

There was a city in ancient Greece, so it is said, where there were two athletes. The city fathers raised a statue in honour of one of them. His rival was consumed with anger. It seems he brooded over what had been done and justified to himself the nightly attack he made upon the statue. Eventually one night he succeeded in knocking the statue down and it fell on him – and killed him. That is what anger does. However natural, however just it is at first, if you hold on to it you destroy yourself.

MEMO

Forgive or fester

Reasons for not forgiving

○ **Punishment**. You can punish by attacking (criticising, scolding, threatening, hitting) or by withdrawing (silence, sulking and insistence on distance). You can punish by rubbing it in and making her feel guilty, or by telling her misdeeds to others so she goes down in their estimation. Forgiveness would mean putting a stop to all that, and as you do not want to stop it you will not forgive.

○ **Protection**. He said, 'If I forgive I am making myself vulnerable to being hurt all over again.'

○ **Prolonging**. The unforgiving is dragged out as long as possible. She said, 'He hasn't suffered enough yet.' By withholding forgiveness you justify (to yourself) your continued hostility.

○ **Prevention**. He did not want to rebuild his marriage so when he said, 'I *can't* forgive', he was saying in effect that the pain was too great and no one could possibly expect him to forgive. That let him off the hook – so he thought.

○ **Pride**. Because of what she has done you feel superior. You can look down on her with contempt. When you forgive you are on the same level as she is and you do not want that.

SUPPOSING ...

○ **Suppose he does not admit that he was wrong?** Either because he is not aware that there is a problem or because he is aware and sees no wrong in it. If you do not forgive until he admits he is wrong you may have a long time to wait. So you probably choose to let it go.

○ **Suppose she does not say 'sorry'?** She excuses or justifies what she did. Wait for the 'sorry' to come and you may wait in vain. So what do you do? You talk it through and if her view is still the same and if it is not a big issue, again you probably let it go.

○ **Suppose there is little or no change?** He said sorry for what he did but he goes on doing it. Well, it depends how serious it is. Say it is a matter of being late. After 20 years of marriage he is better but not much. There is a degree of selfishness, but if his lateness is the worst thing about him you are not going to leave him. You swallow hard and choose if need be to live with it.

But let us say there is adultery or violence or some other extremely abusive situation. There are plenty of excuses but no sorrow, or if there is sorrow there is no change. The violent outbursts continue; he will not give up the affair. Do you let *that* go? If you did, it really would be condoning it. You confront him and spell out the consequences. If there is still no change there may have to be separation or divorce. Further down the line, maybe much further, you may be able to forgive. That may not mean reconciliation, but it will mean that you refuse to become embittered. He may not change; you do. In your heart you forgive and you walk free.

Manner of forgiveness

O **Acknowledge your own contribution**. If you have contributed to the situation then say so.

O **Try to understand your partner**. There is a saying, 'To understand everything is to forgive everything.' There is a measure of truth in this. Was she particularly vulnerable just then? Was the situation in which he found himself difficult? Was her health causing problems, or was he just plain exhausted?

O **Do it privately**. If others are present, do not embarrass him by talking about his failures – even if you are forgiving them!

O **Choose your words**. The words 'I forgive you' can sound pompous. Besides he may not think he needs forgiveness. You may not even use the word for what matters is the attitude of the heart. But of course if he comes to you and asks, 'Will you forgive me?' that is another matter. He wants to hear, 'Yes, I do.'

REMEMBER THE THREE 'A's OF FORGIVENESS

O **Admit**. You admit that what you said or did or failed to do was wrong. The origin of marriage problems is rarely, if ever, one-sided. It maybe 50/50, 60/40, 70/30, 80/20, but not 100/0. You are not responsible for your partner's failures; you are for yours. It is just plain honesty to admit first to yourself and then to your partner, 'I was wrong.'

O **Apologise**. You say sorry for the wrong you did and the hurt you caused. There are those, often with very low self-esteem, who say sorry for everything, and those who say sorry for nothing, perhaps because they never heard the word when they were young. But a genuine apology is not only sensible – you admit to the wrong you did – but also sensitive – you are sorry about the pain it caused. An apology is not a sign of weakness but of strength – strength of mind to see it and strength of character to say it.

If it takes strength to make the apology it is just plain sense to accept it. 'I don't believe you're a bit sorry' hardly makes for more apologies! If there is doubt about the genuineness of the apology, give your partner the benefit of the doubt.

Apology is a sign of strength not weakness

MEMO

O **Alter**. You alter your behaviour so as not to repeat the wrong. Or at least you try. If it is true that the proof of the pudding is in the eating, it is also true that the proof of the apology is in the change, or at least the genuine attempt at it. If a person is really trying to change it is, of course, easier to forgive.

A wife and husband who are going to be best friends and enjoy a really deep companionship, will learn that a good marriage is made up of two people who are not only *givers* of themselves, but also *forgivers* of each other.

Forgiveness brings peace to your marriage. Unselfishness brings joy …

Communication
Affection
Respect
Encouragement
Forgiveness

Unselfishness

Loyalty

Unselfishness

brings joy to your marriage
money, time and habits, likes and dislikes,
roles and responsibilities, the chicken and the egg

'My needs … your duties' is the slogan of the selfish, and 'My duties … your needs' is the cry of the slave. Both are a travesty of the partnership marriage is meant to be. Unselfishness is the foundation on which the whole structure of a good marriage is built. *Nothing* is more important, for where that is present everything else falls into place.

The biblical saying, 'Love your neighbour as yourself' (Mark 12:31) is much misunderstood. It is not *more* than yourself (or less) but *as* yourself. You are to 'Do to others what you would have them do to you' (Matt. 7:12). If one partner in a marriage is too unselfish it can actually contribute to the other being selfish, but if both are unselfish then there will be no dictator and no doormat. Mutual unselfishness is the secret of mutual joy.

MEMO

'Love your neighbour as yourself'

Unselfishness is shown in:

Use of time

Time is the most valuable commodity in life and how you spend it says something about you. If you use time well in marriage you are on your way to getting many other things right. Remember what seems *urgent* may not in fact be *important*.

○ **Parents.** There may be older parents to be cared for. Whether they live on their own or not they need time and love, and getting the balance right is not easy. Whatever short-term emergencies may have to be dealt with, in the long term it should be partner before parent.

○ **Hobbies**. A hobby, which can relax and invigorate, can also divide. A wife whose husband came close to the top of his chosen sport complained, 'I think you love that ball more than me.' Another husband, who found that the training and practice required for playing at the top level was robbing him of time with his wife and family, settled for playing at a lower level. The way he put it was, 'Less practice, better marriage.'

○ **Faith**. There is clear evidence that a meaningful faith and the shared values which go with it can be a powerful influence for stability and enjoyment in marriage. To go into marriage with the same outlook makes a lot of sense. But what happens if during the marriage one partner changes? That is where mutual respect comes in. A husband remarked, 'I don't have her faith but I respect her for it,' and his wife declared, 'We don't let the differences divide us.'

○ **Friends**. Some feel the need of friends and doing things outside home. For others nothing is more attractive than being at home. One wants in and the other out. The sociably minded may be happiest when the telephone rings and friends drop in. But for the quieter one that may not come naturally. Unselfishness means, however, that they accept the differences and deliberately try to adjust to each other's needs.

○ **Work**. Getting the balance right between work and marriage is never easy. On the one hand there is the duty of providing for your home and on the other the importance of protecting your relationship. But one thing is certain: no one on their death-bed says, 'I wish I had spent more time at work.'

- **You encourage by putting your marriage before your work**. There will always be times when, short-term, the demands of work simply must be met. There is no option. But if the long-term demands of work rob a couple of time and energy to such an extent that their relationship suffers, then serious questions need to be asked about the job. One wife complained, 'I wish my husband didn't make so much money,' for she would have preferred less money and more husband. Let your partner know that they are valued even more than your work.

- **You encourage by leaving your work attitudes behind**. One teacher of small children, without realising it, treated her husband like a child, correcting him in the same tone of voice she used during the day. A boss, used to giving instructions in the office, came home and told his wife to get someone for him on the telephone. She replied, 'Get him yourself!' Leadership at work is not a licence for bossiness at home.

- **You encourage by appreciating the work done in your home**. Women used to be asked, 'Are you a housewife or do you work?' But no longer. Cooking, washing, ironing, cleaning, shopping, driving, mending, tidying, organising, even for just two people, *is* work. With a family it is hard labour! Spell out your appreciation loud and clear.

Personal issues

O **Habits**. What do you bring into marriage more than anything else? Habits. Some are bad and need to be changed and some are good and should not be. Some are neither good nor bad. He puts things away when he is finished; she leaves them around. She switches on the TV to watch a particular programme; he channel-hops. She likes plenty of fresh air and is a window-opener; he is a window-closer. His little quirks are annoying to her not necessarily because they are wrong but because they are the opposite of her little quirks.

In a good marriage a couple adjust to each other. One husband when he married was very particular about time. When he said, 'Eight o'clock' he meant eight o'clock, not one minute past eight. It was a statement. When his wife said, 'Eight o'clock' it was a hope. It might mean anything. But they were basically unselfish people and in trying to please each other she eventually became more punctual and he more relaxed about time.

○ **Addictions**. An addict is at first selfish and in the end a slave. Addiction has its price. Time, money, health and even sanity – yours and your partner's. Be honest and, if you have a problem, admit it. Then do something about it. If you cannot overcome it then look for help and do not wait until you are beyond help. No relationship can flourish when there is addiction.

You get what you tolerate

MEMO

If you are married to someone who has an addiction which is significantly affecting your lives, then *you* get help, for your sake as well as his (or hers). It may be necessary to set limits, spell out consequences, have separate bank accounts, cancel credit cards. You are responsible *to* each other, not *for* each other. You can love him but you cannot change him. *He* must act. Remember, you get what you tolerate and if you tolerate the addiction then *you* are part of the problem.

O **Appearance**. If you are both sloppy joes that is fine. But if how you look matters to your partner, take that seriously. Do not let him be disappointed when he looks at you. Look after yourself so she continues to be attracted to you. Turn yourself out so that he is proud of you.

O **Communication**. Do not interrupt. Dale Carnegie laughed, 'If you have an idea when the other fellow is talking, do not wait for him to finish. He is not as smart as you. Why waste your time listening to his idle chatter? Bust right in and interrupt him in the middle of the sentence.' Enough said!

O **Control**. Your partner is a person, not a puppet. Being a controller is not only a sign of selfishness but usually a sign of weakness. A healthy personality does not need to control and likes to share responsibilities and decisions. So share and share alike.

O **Likes and dislikes**. People tend to see *their* preference as being right. He loved history and when he saw his wife reading novels he thought to himself, 'How can any intelligent human being read such rubbish?' Recovering from an operation, history seemed heavy and his wife persuaded him to try one of her books. He was fascinated by the plot and character study. The author of that book had written 30 others, and later her husband grinned sheepishly and admitted, 'I've read them all.' So with colour or music or food or TV programmes. It is perfectly all right to have likes, but do not let your dislikes rubbish your partner's likes. Try to understand them. *You* might even change!

Roles and responsibilities

There are no absolute rules in homes today and who does what is influenced by employment, work schedules, children, money and health, as well as by ability and preference. There are househusbands as well as housewives, six children and none, fat cats and minimum wage, unemployment, disability and illness. Roles and responsibilities change but it is the way in which you unselfishly discharge them which makes a marriage strong.

○ **House**. In the Western world the man used to be the breadwinner and the woman looked after home and children. Whereas this still happens, many wives today are in the work place as well. Washing, ironing, cleaning and cooking do not have 'wife-only' labels, any more than there is a 'husband-only' stamp on DIY or car care.

○ **Children**. Changing or feeding a new baby in the middle of the night (unless of course the mother is breast-feeding), taking children to school, supervising homework and household shopping all offer plenty of opportunity for sharing. If work schedules mean a father cannot give 50/50 let him give what he can when he can. He needs to share not only the play but also the discipline, and she must not allow her mothering to be so all-encompassing that he feels unneeded.

Money

Some of the greatest problems in marriage are over money and sex. Someone laughed, 'The wife does not think she gets enough of the one and the husband does not think he gets enough of the other!' Whether that is true or not it is certain that many couples find money a cause of conflict.

Question: Who looks after the money?

Answer: Whoever has the most time or skill. But whereas one may have the role of treasurer and do most of the work, both should know the facts of their financial situation. There should be no debts that one partner does not know about.

UNDERSTANDING

○ **'Single' attitude**. It is a big leap from 'my' money to 'our' money, from spending 'What I like when I like' to 'What do *you* think?' Even if a husband and wife have separate bank accounts they are going to have to consult. A man came home proudly showing his wife the new camera he had just bought, and she cried because she knew that meant there would be no new shoes for the children.

○ **Family background**. Wealth and poverty are relative, but in your judgment was your home luxurious, modest or poor? Who handled the money when you were a child? Was the family philosophy 'If you have it spend it' or 'Never buy unless you have it'?

○ **Future plans**. Save or spend? Future security or present enjoyment? One lives for tomorrow, the other for today. Both can be justified but it may take time to understand and adapt to each other.

○ **Giving**. You may have a difference of opinion about whether (or how much) money should be given to church or charity, project or person. If you agree then there is no problem, but if you do not share each other's view then you may have to take the middle ground. Far from being a dirty word, 'compromise' is the road to harmony.

CONSULTING

○ **House or flat**. What size of a house or flat do you really need and where should it be? Is it rent or buy? If you are buying it may well be the biggest single expenditure you will ever make. Make joint decisions. You are going to spend a lot of time there and you both need to feel comfortable with it. If you are setting up in your first home, do you have to furnish every room immediately? Does every item have to be new? What happens if two salaries suddenly become one? Or, perish the thought, none?

○ **Mr and Mrs Jones**. 'Buying things you don't need, with money you don't have, to impress people you don't like' is all too often true. A comfortable home is better than a spotless show house any day. Talk it over together and then set your own standards within your own limits.

○ **Advertising**. The advertisements tell you in effect, 'You can be happy only if you have this product', and a year later they say, 'You can be happy only if you have the new updated version of this product.' Remind each other not to believe them. Think before you buy.

Think before you buy

MEMO

○ **Credit**. Credit cards, hire purchase and catalogue sales are convenient – and can be dangerous. The slogan is, 'Have it now – pay later.' Some pay dearly. Debt or the fear of debt is one of the greatest bones of contention in marriage. Many couples find a useful rule of thumb is: hire purchase for necessities – yes, if affordable; for luxuries – no. If there are money problems some people cut up the cards and go back to cash.

MANAGING

○ **Professional advisors**. Professional advisors on mortgages, life assurance, insurance, pensions, taxation and making a will may save you more than they cost.

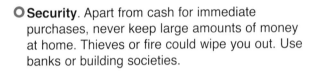

MEMO 'If you fail to plan, you plan to fail'

○ **Security**. Apart from cash for immediate purchases, never keep large amounts of money at home. Thieves or fire could wipe you out. Use banks or building societies.

○ **Budgeting**. There are two good sayings to remember. The first is, 'If you fail to plan, you plan to fail', and the second, 'If your outgoings exceed your income then your upkeep will be your downfall.' Get it down in black and white. It will take time but could save you headaches and heartaches.

The chicken and the egg

When it comes to complaints about selfishness, wives typically point to their husbands' lack of consideration and husbands to their wives' lack of affection. These two are connected. If a husband is inconsiderate and does not help his wife at home and with the children, he is likely to find that his wife is not affectionate. When his wife is not affectionate he loses motivation to be considerate. And so it goes on.

But it can go the other way. The more he unselfishly reaches out to his wife and considers her needs, the easier and more natural she finds it to meet his need for affection, which in turn leads him to want to please and support her. Which comes first, the chicken or the egg? Is it consideration or affection? Wives say consideration, husbands say affection. But mutual and unselfish meeting of each other's needs is fundamental to happiness in marriage.

Where there is unselfishness, time, money and responsibilities are shared, bad habits are broken and good ones formed. Husband and wife move toward each other and stand by each other. Happiness lies with two people who have the one purpose of pleasing each other.

Unselfishness brings joy to your marriage. Loyalty keeps love …

Communication

Affection

Respect

Encouragement

Forgiveness

Unselfishness

Loyalty

Loyalty

keeps love in your marriage
parents, children and friends, how affairs develop,
preventative measures, choosing to trust, to
stay or go

On their wedding day there are couples who exchanged their solemn vows of love with the words 'For better for worse, for richer for poorer, in sickness and in health, until death us do part'. Whether with these words or others, they made a commitment which is as absolute as it is voluntary. Their marriage relationship is to have priority over every other relationship.

Partner and parents

There are those who have been so abused, neglected or rejected by their parents that no bond remains, and perhaps no contact. But for most people marriage does not sever the link with a parent or parents and their approval, and acceptance by in-laws, is important. To keep that relationship enjoyable:

○ **Be separate.** Early in marriage it is best not to be living in the same house as parents or in-laws. The newly married particularly need privacy. Later an elderly parent may need to be taken into their home and looked after, but that is another story.

○ **Be independent**. It is possible to be separate geographically yet not emotionally. For those who have been emotionally dependent on a parent, it may take time to wean themselves away, but a husband needs to feel he comes before his wife's parents and she needs the same assurance with regard to his parents. At the beginning of a marriage it may be unwise to get locked into a tradition with parents (say *always* lunch on Sunday) that it may be hard to break later.

○ **Be considerate**. The fifth commandment, 'Honour your father and your mother' (Exod. 20:12), does not mean that as an adult you have to obey them. But if you have received from one or both of them years of love and support, then you will want to show your gratitude to them. Keeping in touch will mean much to parents who will never (probably *can* never) cease to love you. As they get older and less active they may need a helping-hand in some way. Many parents love to help with grandchildren but you need to take care lest in their availability they feel 'used'.

○ **Be firm**. What a parent sees as kindness may be felt as intrusion, and if this happens it is best for the wife to deal with her parents and the husband with his. 'Thanks for the offer but I think we can handle this ourselves.' Some parents, particularly mothers, find it hard to let go of their adult children even when they are married, and there is a spoken or unspoken demand, 'You owe it to me', that needs to be firmly dealt with.

○ **Be supportive**. Back each other up either in the support that needs to be given to parents or the interference that needs to be resisted. Allow no criticism by a parent of your husband or wife. One couple had his elderly mother living with them during the last years of her life. The husband wrote, 'With my wife and mother in the same house there was the potential for conflict. But there was very little. My rule was, "My wife first, right or wrong." My wife knew that and so she was confident; my mother knew it and never tried to divide us. It may have seemed to some to be unfair – but it worked.'

Partner and children

O **A whole new ball game**. When children come, life changes. One husband said 'When the first baby came I loved him and (I hate to admit it) was jealous of him at the same time. I felt I was no longer the centre of her world. Then there were two more children, and so far as my work allowed, I needed to be right in there with her. Inevitably we had much less time and energy for each other, but because our love for our children was a shared love, and our involvement in their lives a shared involvement, neither of us felt a displaced person.'

O **Getting the balance right**. There are times when the child must come first. When they are very small it can be a life-and-death matter. But equally there are times when the parent should come first, for parents are people too. They also have needs. If a child learns that his wants always get preference, then it is likely he will become an adult who always wants his own way.

O **Backing each other up**. One person looking back on childhood said, 'We could never divide our parents. We certainly tried! But what Dad said, Mum said. What Mum said, Dad said. They didn't always think alike, but to us they spoke with one voice. It gave us a lot of security and we really respected them for their loyalty to each other. They were allies.'

Partner and friends

Most couples have friends, maybe other couples, who enrich their marriage with their banter, sympathy, support or common interests. Wives may have girl friends and husbands mates, and this can help to give the couple an element of space from each other. But in most happy marriages husband and wife are 'best friends' and they ensure that no other relationship intrudes or weakens their friendship. It may mean saying 'no' to friends in order to say 'yes' to each other.

Partner in front of others

Do not knock him in front of others (even if he laughs, he may be hurting inside). Back him up in front of family and friends. If you are talking about her when she is not present, talk her up, not down. You show your loyalty by what you say to each other, or about each other, in front of others.

> **Talk her up, not down** MEMO

Partner and the other man (or woman)

Loyalty is a good word and conveys the idea of two people who are trustworthy and unswerving in their commitment to each other. On their wedding day the great majority of couples promise sexual faithfulness, and breaking their marriage vow they would see as deeply and intrinsically wrong. To sexual unfaithfulness the Bible gives the word 'adultery' and states loud and clear, 'You shall not commit adultery' (Exod. 20:14). It is a wrong not only against husband or wife but a sin against God. How does it happen?

BACKGROUND TO AN AFFAIR

Typically this is what happens. There are:

○ **Shortcomings**. One or both do not put into their relationship those things which make a marriage thrive. Either they have not learned the secrets of a happy marriage or have not carried through with what they know. Then lack of communication, affection, respect and so on brings …

○ **Disappointment**. Not all at once perhaps and at first there is hope that things will get better. But there is increasing frustration with the lack of change so that gradually disappointment becomes …

○ **Resentment**. 'I've given so much and seem to get so little in return. I don't deserve to be treated like this. *I* have needs.' The longer resentment burns the more likely it is to lead to …

○ **Withdrawal**. One or both distance themselves emotionally, and then with lost intimacy there can be escape into job or children. The withdrawal verbally or physically is explained by, 'When I'm hurting like this I just don't want to be close.' Then with withdrawal comes …

○ **Vulnerability**. Though living under the same roof and even sharing the same bed loneliness creeps in. This may go on for a long time but a lonely partner is a vulnerable person.

DEVELOPMENT OF AN AFFAIR

○ **Attraction**. Everyone knows people whose looks, ability or personality they admire. That is inescapable, entirely normal and healthy and mostly it stops there. But if these admired things have an emotional or physical impact, which instead of being dismissed are allowed to be savoured, then a new dimension emerges. 'I'm noticed …' 'I feel appreciated …' 'We laugh a lot …' 'We can talk about anything …' 'There's a chemistry between us.' The attraction (which may be heterosexual or homosexual) grows and is justified by 'I can't help feeling like this.'

O **Rationalisation**. 'I can't help feeling like this and these wonderful warm feelings must be all right.' (Every intelligent adult knows that a warm glow inside is no reliable guide – except when it is your own!). 'We're such good friends, and anyway after the way I've been treated I deserve a break.' 'Nobody knows so nobody will get hurt. We'll not let it go too far.' The rationalisation which justified the developing attraction justifies also the …

> **MYTH:**
> 'These wonderful warm feelings must be all right'

O **Fantasy**. There are daydreams of tenderness and intimacy. He is at first the courteous romantic knight in shining armour and then the irresistible lover who sweeps her off her feet. She is the beautiful girl who becomes the insatiable sexual nymph. The glands control the brains. There are no flaws or faults on either side. It is of course rapturous, ecstatic, idyllic … nonsense. The dream world is not the real world of noise, traffic, chores, bills and responsibilities where real love is put to the test. The old saying that the thought is the father of the deed is proved true when fantasy leads to …

O **Involvement**. Planned or unplanned a line is crossed. Looks are exchanged, words spoken, there is a touch, a hug, a kiss, and then all the way to sexual intercourse. The sense of guilt lessens as the relationship continues, and the present passion may be so intense that love for husband or wife pales before it. But it is hard to stay involved unless there is …

O **Concealment**. Concealment was all that was needed at first but suddenly in order to conceal it is necessary to lie. Then a lie to cover a lie. To tell the truth is unthinkable and so lies seem logical. In the end they come easily. 'Nobody must know. They would be so hurt and angry and what we are doing would have to stop.' Deception becomes routine.

The development of the affair can be telescoped into days or less or spread over months and years.

AFTERMATH OF AN AFFAIR

O **Discovery**. An unguarded word, intuitive suspicion, a story that does not hang together, coldness and indifference noticed and challenged. There are probing questions and indignant denials, 'Of course not! We're just friends. Don't you trust me?' A lie is found out and at first only what is discovered is admitted, or a little is confessed to hide the greater. Then more questions – Who? Where? What? When? Sometimes the affair is admitted voluntarily with 'I had to get it off my chest'.

O **Damage**. Some say that an affair is good for a marriage. That is a mega myth. Even if the affair comes to an end and never comes to light, standards have been lowered and conscience weakened. Getting away with it may lead to chancing it with someone else. Where it does become known there is unimaginable pain. 'I couldn't believe this was happening to me …' 'I cried for weeks …' 'I walked around in a daze …' 'I felt like a raging animal …' 'I didn't want to live.' The scars can remain for years, sometimes for life.

○ **Confrontation**. 'I know I may not be able to hold your love but one thing is certain: it's either her or me. You can't have both. If you continue with this affair then that's an end to our marriage. If I'm convinced the affair is over and you are serious about our marriage, then I'll think about it. But it's going to take a long time to trust again. For me it's total commitment or nothing. You have a choice to make.'

The confrontation may lead to separation and divorce. Sometimes there is no alternative. Or it may begin the often slow process of rebuilding. The bricks used in rebuilding are the same as those which should have been used in the first place in the building of the marriage – communication, affection, respect and so on. It can happen that because the couple so nearly lost their marriage they come to value it even more. One wife wrote, 'I would not want to live through that again, but what happened made us face issues as never before. I never thought I would ever be able to say this but we have a marriage now which is better than ever.'

> **MEGA MYTH:**
> An affair is good for marriage

ENDING AN AFFAIR

○ **Breaking it off**. Seldom is an affair broken off without pain especially if only one party wants to end it. With the rejection there will be anger. Tears, recrimination, a plea for one last hug – and the whole thing can start again. One man could not trust himself to break it off in private and so did it while walking in a public place. A woman, having decided she had to end the affair face to face, confided in a girl friend what she was going to do, and immediately after the confrontation she telephoned her friend and told her what she had done.

O **Disposing of the symbols**. If there have been gifts received during the affair it is important to get rid of them. If the affair and the gifts were known to husband or wife then any gifts, letters or photographs retained will still be a constant source of friction. But even if the affair was unknown anything kept will be a link with the past. So a man gave away to a charity shop the clothes he had received; a woman destroyed the letters that she had so carefully preserved. Both said that until they had done this they were not fully free.

O **Being resolute**. Once a relationship has been sexual it is not possible to be 'just friends' again. The best policy is no contact whatsoever – even by letter, email, telephone or text. If because of a work situation contact is inevitable then it should be only what is absolutely necessarily professionally. If a wife (say) knows of the affair, her husband should undertake that, if ever the other woman tries to contact him or they meet accidentally, he will immediately tell her. If he fails to do so, and his wife learns of it later, she may feel he is hiding something.

PREVENTING AN AFFAIR

O **Keeping it fresh**. The best way to prevent an affair is to develop a marriage which is held together not only by solemn commitment but also by a relationship so good that neither would want to spoil it. The marriage is fun. Wife and husband affirm and support each other, and vie with each other to see how much they can give. Through tears and laughter they are together. She is Number One to him and he to her. With a marriage and a love like this there is no room or wish for a third party.

○ **Go easy on criticism**. A husband who later deeply regretted his adultery said, 'I'm not justifying what I did. It was wrong. But I need my wife to understand that after years of the acid rain of her criticism I found someone who accepted me. And I fell for it.' To her credit after an initial, 'I only said those things for his good', she realised what she had done in driving her husband away.

○ **Alerting to danger**. A wife described how a man made a pass at her at work. She was mildly flattered but told the man she did not appreciate it. She told her husband what had happened and later the man concerned that she had told her husband. He never did it again and her husband's confidence in her soared.

A husband felt the impact of an attractive girl at work and after struggling with his feelings for a while decided, with some embarrassment, to tell his wife. She was less than happy, but both were glad of the openness which made it possible for him to speak. He said from that moment on he did not have a problem with his feelings, and he proved the truth that in secrecy there is weakness and in openness strength.

In secrecy weakness, in openness strength

MEMO

○ **Avoiding the situation**. If you want to save yourself injury or worse it is just plain sense to walk on the pavement and not in the middle of the road. Maintaining loyalty to each other may mean declining an invitation, reorganising a lift to work, or refusing to respond to someone's requests for help. It will mean caution about meeting people on the Internet. Faithfulness is a choice and therefore avoid the situation, the person, the place, the conversation which might lead down the road to 'I couldn't help myself.' Be blunt if necessary.

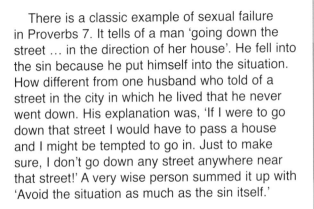

Avoid the situation as much as the sin itself

There is a classic example of sexual failure in Proverbs 7. It tells of a man 'going down the street … in the direction of her house'. He fell into the sin because he put himself into the situation. How different from one husband who told of a street in the city in which he lived that he never went down. His explanation was, 'If I were to go down that street I would have to pass a house and I might be tempted to go in. Just to make sure, I don't go down any street anywhere near that street!' A very wise person summed it up with 'Avoid the situation as much as the sin itself.'

○ **Considering the consequences**. If the affair comes to light there is anguish, sometimes so great that it can lead to mental and emotional breakdown. A husband, whose one-night stand was discovered by his wife, said 'A few minutes of doubtful pleasure for me and years of pain for my wife. It was by far the most stupid thing I ever did.' Another husband had no idea that his wife had had various sexual liaisons until tell-tale signs showed he had a serious sexual disease. He was devastated not merely by his wife's adultery but by the deceit which surrounded it.

(For the consequences for children and the wider circle see below under 'To stay or go').

To trust or not to trust

- **Early years**. To grow up in an atmosphere of loyalty and dependability makes it easier to trust in adult years.

- **Personal experience**. The nature of relationships in the years between childhood and marriage can make for trust or otherwise.

- **Partner's behaviour**. Flirty behaviour or affairs obviously make it very difficult to trust. Many have said that they find it harder to trust than to forgive.

- **Trust and naivety**. Trust is good but not blind trust which will not face the evidence.

- **Trust is a choice**. A girl engaged to be married had only to see her fiancé talking to another girl in a crowd for her to be overwhelmed by suspicion. Behind that suspicion was a father who had betrayed her mother's trust, and on his remarriage his second wife had betrayed his trust. When a counsellor suggested that she postpone her wedding until she was able to deal with the problem she realised she had a choice to make. She said, 'I decided to trust.' Many years later, and happy with husband and children, she regarded that resolve as the turning point of her life.

To stay or go

This is an era where, if a machine does not work properly, it is easier and often cheaper to get a new one rather than repair the old one. But people are not machines and there is ample evidence to show that it is usually much easier (and a lot cheaper!) to repair a marriage than dispose of it.

Sometimes nothing can be done; one partner just leaves, and that is that. Or the behaviour is so unreasonable that there is no realistic hope of saving the marriage. But of those who separate for what are called 'irreconcilable differences', a surprising number say later, 'We could have worked it out.'

WHAT ARE THE REASONS FOR STAYING?

○ **For your own sake**. Parting can be costly when there are lawyers, courts and financial obligations. Perhaps two households to provide for instead of one. If wives and husbands choose to part they very often do not part as friends, yet if there are children they may have to do business with each other for years over money, access and education.

   Loneliness, bitterness and depression are common experiences. The instance of psychiatric treatment among the divorced is significantly higher than among the married. Even if life is shared with another partner, second marriages break down more often than first, third marriages more often than second, and cohabitation more frequently than remarriage.

○ **For the children's sake**. Parents rarely part without pain and sometimes indescribable anguish for the children. No one can predict the long-term effects for a particular child, but there is overwhelming evidence to show that when parents part the children are *more likely* to have lower standards of education, to break up if they cohabit or divorce if they marry, to be sexually abused, to be involved in domestic violence and in crime, and to have emotional and psychological problems as adults. There are many wonderful exceptions to these terrible statistics but the trend is clear.

○ **For the wider circle**. Friendships are broken. The wife (say) may find that after a while her married women friends begin to back away because they see *her* as a potential threat to *their* marriages. Families take sides. Like it or not, grandparents are often involved in extra childminding and *their* lives may be turned upside down.

Loyalty keeps love in your marriage.

○ **Choose how you feel.** All that has been said involves choices. They are things you do. You cannot actually make yourself have loving feelings (or any other feelings for that matter). But you can directly control your thoughts, words and actions. These are the things that change your feelings positively or negatively. What you think, say and do powerfully influence how you feel. The CAREFUL factors are the soil in which love grows, the foundation on which the house of marriage is built.

○ **Grow in love.** People who say 'I don't love him (or her) any more' often make the mistake of comparing the present to the 'in love' feelings they had when (or before) they were married. But the fantastic 'cloud nine' feelings do not last. A husband explains, 'When I first held her hand it took about a week for my hand to recover from the thrill. Now that I have held her hand (and a lot more) a few thousand times, there isn't the same excitement. But you can keep "cloud nine". We have instead an intimacy and an incredible oneness. We *fell* in love quickly enough, but far more fulfilling has been the way we have been *growing* in love.'

○ **Keep learning.** A very happily married couple wrote, 'We learned from our mistakes and tried not to repeat them. We learned from watching other marriages and what seemed to make them strong or weak. We learned from a wealth of written material on relationships so we became students of marriage as well as of each other. But most of all we learned from the things that worked for us and built on them.'

O **Take responsibility**. Never take your marriage or each other for granted. Remember that the only person you can change is yourself. Work on that. Take responsibility for your own happiness. Stay interesting. A certain sameness is natural in marriage – the same two people – but sameness does not have to mean staleness. Try new things; keep your mind exercised as well as your body; develop as a person; tackle bad habits and aim to overcome them; be positive; be good at something. Even if your husband or wife does not change as much as you would like, you will feel comfortable with what *you* are, and *that* will affect your marriage.

The only person you can change is yourself

MEMO

O **Build a team spirit**. Regard your marriage as a team and put the good of the team first. He makes her problem his. She is glad when he does well. Let 'we' come before 'me'. If there is a clash between the interests of the team and the individual, the team comes first. What is good for the team is good for both members of it.

O **Persevere**. Where two rivers meet there is often rough water and turbulence until the two rivers become one, and flow deeper, quieter and stronger. And when two lives come together there can be rough water until the two lives merge into a deeper and stronger union. But it takes time. Persevere.

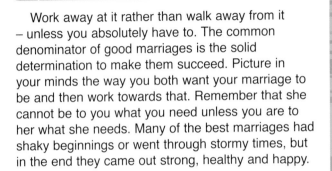

MEMO

'We' before 'me'.

Work away at it rather than walk away from it – unless you absolutely have to. The common denominator of good marriages is the solid determination to make them succeed. Picture in your minds the way you both want your marriage to be and then work towards that. Remember that she cannot be to you what you need unless you are to her what she needs. Many of the best marriages had shaky beginnings or went through stormy times, but in the end they came out strong, healthy and happy.

- **C**ommunication brings light
- **A**ffection brings warmth
- **R**espect brings dignity
- **E**ncouragement brings hope
- **F**orgiveness brings peace
- **U**nselfishness brings joy
- **L**oyalty keeps love

Remember good marriages do not just happen – they are made.

If you are in the middle of a muddle in your marriage look for help … soon. Small weeds come out easily because they have shallow roots. A car properly serviced is less likely to let you down. It is best to go to the doctor when symptoms first appear. Do not wait until your marriage needs intensive care!

○ **Read a good book**. There tend to be two kinds of books on marriage, one dealing with the whole of the relationship and the other specifically with sex. You could read together side by side, or he a bit and she a bit and talking it over as you go through it. You may be able to resolve your problems without anyone knowing you had any. If you are trying to make your marriage work you will obviously choose books which are pro-marriage.

○ **Go to a good model**. It is possible to be influenced negatively by friends who have had their own problems in marriage, and there are plenty of examples of those who have shared their difficulties with someone of the opposite sex (say at work) and it has multiplied the problems. But if you know a couple who seem to have a really good marriage, why not say to them, 'Tell us how you did it'? If they have the kind of marriage you think they have, they will probably be delighted to share what they have found.

○ **Sign up for a course**. There are many courses on marriage and marriage preparation, most of which are led by people who have had a lot of personal experience – and who probably faced many difficulties in gaining that experience. The comments from those attending such courses are frequently, 'We never knew there was so much to discover.'

O **Go to a professional**. If you want your marriage to work you could go to a counsellor. You may have to pay but it could be the best investment you ever made. One or two visits might do the trick but it is more likely it will take a number of weeks or months depending on the nature of the problems. If you both really work at it you make the counsellor's job easier and it is much quicker. Churches may be able to help or they may point to someone who can. 'We have come from despair to happiness beyond anything we ever thought possible' was the testimony of one couple who went for counselling, and those words have been echoed by thousands.

National Distributors

UK: (and countries not listed below)
CWR, Waverley Abbey House, Waverley Lane, Farnham, Surrey
GU9 8EP. Tel: (01252) 784700 Outside UK (44) 1252 784700

AUSTRALIA: CMC Australasia, PO Box 519, Belmont, Victoria
3216. Tel: (03) 5241 3288 Fax: (03) 5241 3290

CANADA: David C Cook Distribution Canada, PO Box 98, 55
Woodslee Avenue, Paris, Ontario N3L 3E5. Tel: 1800 263 2664

GHANA: Challenge Enterprises of Ghana, PO Box 5723, Accra.
Tel: (021) 222437/223249 Fax: (021) 226227

HONG KONG: Cross Communications Ltd, 1/F, 562A Nathan Road,
Kowloon. Tel: 2780 1188 Fax: 2770 6229

INDIA: Crystal Communications, 10-3-18/4/1, East Marredpalli,
Secunderabad – 500026, Andhra Pradesh. Tel/Fax: (040) 27737145

KENYA: Keswick Books and Gifts Ltd, PO Box 10242-00400,
Nairobi. Tel: (254) 20 312639/3870125

MALAYSIA: Salvation Book Centre (M) Sdn Bhd, 23 Jalan SS 2/64,
47300 Petaling Jaya, Selangor. Tel: (03) 78766411/78766797 Fax: (03)
78757066/78756360

Canaanland, No. 25 Jalan PJU 1A/41B, NZX Commercial Centre, Ara
Jaya, 47301 Petaling Jaya, Selangor. Tel: (03) 7885 0540/1/2 Fax: (03)
7885 0545

NEW ZEALAND: CMC Australasia, PO Box 303298, North
Harbour, Auckland 0751. Tel: 0800 449 408 Fax: 0800 449 049

NIGERIA: FBFM, Helen Baugh House, 96 St Finbarr's College Road,
Akoka, Lagos. Tel: (01) 7747429/4700218/825775/827264

PHILIPPINES: OMF Literature Inc, 776 Boni Avenue,
Mandaluyong City. Tel: (02) 531 2183 Fax: (02) 531 1960

SINGAPORE: Alby Commercial Enterprises Pte Ltd, 95 Kallang
Avenue #04-00, AIS Industrial Building, 339420. Tel: (65) 629 27238
Fax: (65) 629 27235

SOUTH AFRICA: Struik Christian Books, 80 MacKenzie Street, PO
Box 1144, Cape Town 8000. Tel: (021) 462 4360 Fax: (021) 461 3612

SRI LANKA: Christombu Publications (Pvt) Ltd, Bartleet House, 65
Braybrooke Place, Colombo 2. Tel: (9411) 2421073/2447665

USA: David C Cook Distribution Canada, PO Box 98, 55 Woodslee
Avenue, Paris, Ontario N3L 3E5, Canada. Tel: 1800 263 2664

For email addresses, visit the CWR website: www.cwr.org.uk
CWR is a Registered Charity — Number 294387
CWR is a Limited Company registered in England — Registration
Number 1990308

Day and Residential Courses
Counselling Training
Leadership Development
Biblical Study Courses
Regional Seminars
Ministry to Women
Daily Devotionals
Books and Videos
Conference Centre

Trusted all Over the World

CWR HAS GAINED A WORLDWIDE reputation as a centre of excellence for Bible-based training and resources. From our headquarters at Waverley Abbey House, Farnham, England, we have been serving God's people for over 40 years with a vision to help apply God's Word to everyday life and relationships. The daily devotional *Every Day with Jesus* is read by nearly a million readers an issue in more than 150 countries, and our unique courses in biblical studies and pastoral care are respected all over the world. Waverley Abbey House provides a conference centre in a unique setting.

For free brochures on our seminars and courses, conference facilities, or a catalogue of CWR resources, please contact us at the following address. **CWR, Waverley Abbey House, Waverley Lane, Farnham, Surrey GU9 8EP, UK**

Telephone: **+44 (0)1252 784700**
Email: **mail@cwr.org.uk**
Website: **www.cwr.org.uk**

Preparation for Marriage

Weekends for those engaged or planning to be married

Building the right, biblical foundation for your marriage is so important. What better way to do that than to take some time out together for a CWR *Preparation for Marriage* weekend. Key features:

- What is a Christian marriage?
- Understanding love and loving, sex and sexuality
- The basic cause of marriage breakdown and how to avoid it
- Evaluating strengths, weaknesses and potential stress points
- The three types of love in marriage
- Why conflict occurs and how to handle it
- Understanding your temperaments through the Myers Briggs™ Type Indicator

*'An excellent weekend.
Lots of laughs too!'*

CWR also offer a Marriage on Track course for those already married.

For dates/further details on this and other seminars/courses please contact us at:
Waverley Training and Events, CWR, Waverley Abbey House, Waverley Lane, Farnham, Surrey GU9 8EP
T: 01252 784719 **E:** training@cwr.org.uk
www.cwr.org.uk

CWR

The Highway Code for Parenting

This *Highway Code* book is a parent guide with a difference. It's about love and esteem, discipline and development of character. This is for those about to become parents; those feeling overwhelmed, struggling with issues, or simply wanting to enjoy their family more.

ISBN: 978-1-85345-419-6
£6.99 (plus p&p)

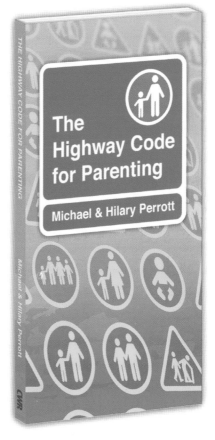

Happiness is a serious business

Some people have everything, yet are miserable. Others who have little or nothing are content and full of life. Why is this?

In the third of the highly readable and practical *Highway Code* series, the authors draw on their many years of counselling experience, and laughingly contend that 'happiness is a serious business'.

ISBN: 978-1-85345-485-1
£6.99 (plus p&p)

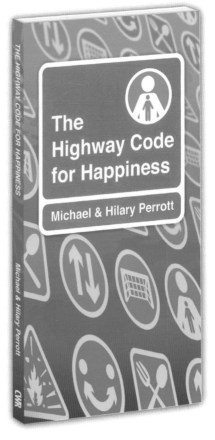

Price correct at time of printing.